CORAL REEFS

by Sylvia A. Johnson

Photographs by Shohei Shirai

A Lerner Natural Science Book

Lerner Publications Company ▪ Minneapolis

Sylvia A. Johnson, Series Editor

Translation of original text by Chaim Uri

The publisher wishes to thank Franklin H. Barnwell, Associate Professor, Department of Ecology and Behavioral Biology, University of Minnesota, for his assistance in the preparation of this book.

Additional photographs courtesy of: p. 11, Brian Parker, Tom Stack & Associates; pp. 20, 50, Carter M. Ayres; p. 42, Franklin H. Barnwell; p. 45, A. Kerstich (lower left), Ed Robinson (lower right), Tom Stack & Associates; p. 47, Atsushi Sakurai (upper left and right), S. Arthur Reed (lower)

Drawings by David Barnard

A note on scientific classification can be found on page 52. The glossary on pages 54 and 55 gives definitions and pronunciations of words shown in **bold type** in the text.

LIBRARY OF CONGRESS CATALOGING IN PUBLICATION DATA

Johnson, Sylvia A.
   Coral reefs.

   (A Lerner natural science book)
   Adaptation of: Sangoshō no sekai / by Shōhei Shirai.
   Includes index.
   Summary: Text and photographs examine the different kinds of coral reefs and their composition and describe the variety of fish, mollusks, crustaceans, and other animals that live in the reef environment.
   1. Coral reef biology — Juvenile literature.
2. Corals — Juvenile literature. 3. Coral reefs and islands — Juvenile literature. [1. Coral reef biology.
2. Corals. 3. Marine animals 4. Coral reefs and islands] I. Shirai, Shōhei, 1933-   , ill.
II. Shirai, Shōhei, 1933-   . Sangoshō no sekai.
III. Title. IV. Series.
QH95.8.J64   1984   574.92   84-816
ISBN 0-8225-1451-6 (lib. bdg.)

This edition first published 1984 by Lerner Publications Company.
Text copyright © 1984 by Lerner Publications Company.
Photographs copyright © 1975 by Shohei Shirai.
Text adapted from CORAL REEFS copyright © 1975 by Shohei Shirai.
English language rights arranged by Kurita-Bando Literary Agency
for Akane Shobo Publishers, Tokyo, Japan.

All rights to this edition reserved by Lerner Publications Company.
International copyright secured. Manufactured in the United States of America.

International Standard Book Number: 0-8225-1451-6
Library of Congress Catalog Card Number: 84-816

1 2 3 4 5 6 7 8 9 10 93 92 91 90 89 88 87 86 85 84

It is hard to imagine any natural environment more fascinating or more mysterious than a coral reef. Submerged in the clear, shallow waters of the world's tropical oceans, reefs are enormous limestone structures teeming with strange forms of life. Animals that look like waving fans or flowering plants; fish marked with zebra stripes or neon colors; worms that live in tubes and snails that kill with deadly poison—coral reefs are home to these and many other exotic creatures.

One of the inhabitants of a coral reef is an animal so small and inconspicuous that its presence could easily be overlooked. Yet this tiny creature — the coral polyp — is responsible for the existence of the whole complicated reef community.

Waves break over a coral reef surrounding an island in the Pacific Ocean. The enormous reef structure is the creation of tiny animals called coral polyps.

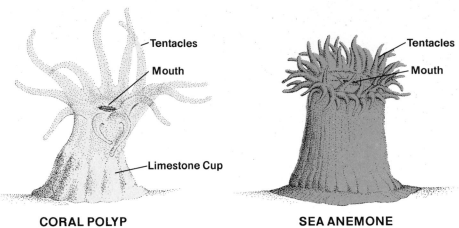

CORAL POLYP   **SEA ANEMONE**

As animals go, coral polyps are very simple creatures. Compared to mammals like cats and humans or even to fish, polyps have only a few parts to their bodies. A polyp's body consists basically of a kind of tube made out of jelly-like tissue. At one end of the tube is an opening or mouth that is used to take in food and to expel waste material. This opening is surrounded by a number of hollow, flexible **tentacles**, which serve to carry food into the polyp's body. Inside the body is a cavity where food is digested.

Coral polyps are similar to another kind of soft-bodied sea creature, the sea anemone. Both belong to the scientific group or phylum called **Coelenterata**, a name taken from two Greek words meaning "hollow gut." Although the coral polyp has the same basic body structure as its relative, it has some characteristics that are different from the anemone and other coelenterates. One of the most significant is the ability of many polyps to produce hard limestone as a protection for their soft bodies.

This greatly enlarged photograph shows coral polyps with their tube-like bodies and long tentacles. The polyps are only 1/5 inch (5 millimeters) in diameter.

The limestone cups, or coral-lites, produced by coral polyps. This photograph clearly shows the sharp-edged partitions, called septa, that divide each corallite.

Limestone is a rocky material made up of a chemical compound called **calcium carbonate**. The ocean contains calcium carbonate in dissolved form, and coral polyps are able to extract it from the ocean water. The cells in the outer layers of their bodies are equipped to perform this specialized work.

After extracting calcium carbonate from the sea, a polyp usually deposits layers of the material around the lower half of its body so that it forms a kind of cup. A polyp can pull its whole body, including its long tentacles, inside the limestone cup, or **corallite**. The hard material provides a secure shelter for the soft and vulnerable animal.

Coral polyps that are capable of forming protective limestone skeletons are referred to as **stony corals**, and they are the primary builders of a coral reef. The process by which these tiny individual polyps create reefs the size of mountains is remarkable and complex.

This coral reef is made up of the limestone skeletons of many different stony corals.

A new reef is usually started by a single polyp that is the offspring of fully developed polyps already established in a reef. This new polyp is created by **sexual reproduction**, or the union of male and female sex cells. In some kinds of stony corals, there are separate male and female polyps, while in others, polyps are capable of producing both male and female reproductive cells.

When a polyp produces male cells, or sperm, it expels them into the water. The sperm are then taken into the bodies of polyps that have produced female cells, or eggs. Here the reproductive cells unite to form immature polyps, called **planulae**.

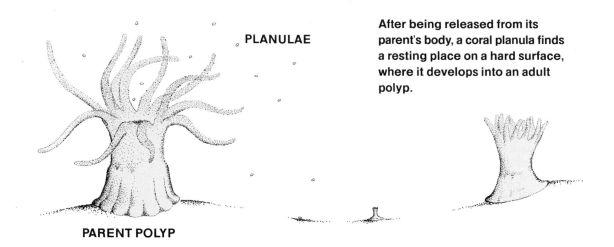

PLANULAE

After being released from its parent's body, a coral planula finds a resting place on a hard surface, where it develops into an adult polyp.

PARENT POLYP

Released from their parent's body through the mouth opening, the tiny planulae swim through the ocean water for several hours or days. During this time, their lives are constantly threatened by the many marine predators that feed on undeveloped polyps and other young sea creatures.

If a planula survives this early period of its life, it eventually finds a resting place on some hard surface no more than 150 feet (45 meters) beneath sea level. Once settled, it immediately begins producing limestone to attach itself permanently to its new home and to protect its soft body. Hidden in its limestone shelter, the planula completes its development and becomes a mature coral polyp.

Once a polyp has established itself, it quickly begins producing other polyps that will share its new living space. These polyps are created not through sexual reproduction but by means of an **asexual** or nonsexual process that does not involve the union of special sex cells.

9

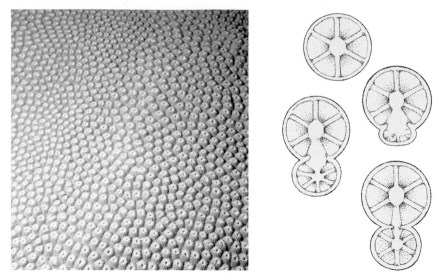

Colonies of stony corals (left) are often formed by the process of budding (right).

Asexual reproduction usually takes place through the process of **budding.** In some kinds of corals, a new polyp appears as a bud or outgrowth on the body tissue of the original polyp. The bud gradually develops into an independent polyp with its own corallite adjoining that of its parent. (This process is shown in the drawings above.) In another form of budding, the new polyp develops on a thin layer of connective tissue that extends out from the body of the original polyp.

Through budding and other forms of asexual reproduction, individual polyps can multiply until they create whole **coral colonies**. A coral colony is a kind of limestone apartment house containing thousands of inhabitants. The colony members occupy adjoining accommodations and cooperate with their neighbors in carrying on all the functions of their lives.

Coral colonies on the Great Barrier Reef

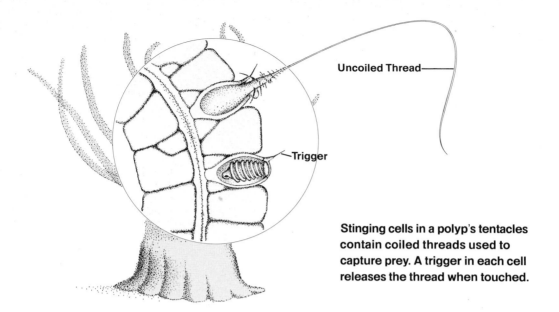

Uncoiled Thread

Trigger

Stinging cells in a polyp's tentacles contain coiled threads used to capture prey. A trigger in each cell releases the thread when touched.

One of the most important tasks carried out by the coral polyps in a colony is obtaining food from the ocean waters. Polyps are meat-eaters, feeding on the immature forms of other sea animals such as shrimps, crabs, lobsters, and fish. These tiny creatures are known as **zooplankton**, a word that means "wandering animals." Millions of zooplankton drift through ocean waters, and many never live long enough to finish their own development and become adults.

A coral polyp captures a meal of zooplankton by using special stinging cells on its tentacles. These cells, called **nematocysts**, contain coiled threads that discharge poison. When drifting zooplankton brush against a polyp's extended tentacles, the threads shoot out and stun the tiny animals with a dose of poison. Then the tentacles carry the zooplankton into the polyp's mouth, which is connected to the digestive cavity inside its body.

The polyps in this colony of galaxea coral *(Galaxea fascicularis)* have their tentacles extended. The tentacles of coral polyps are equipped with stinging cells used to capture food.

In their search for food, the polyps in this colony of daisy coral have extended their soft bodies far outside their protective limestone cups. Most kinds of stony corals feed only during the nighttime hours, but the daisy coral *(Goniopora minor)* also emerges to feed during the day.

Coral colonies take many strange forms. The colony on the left is shaped like a vase or chalice, while the one on the right resembles short, stubby fingers. The scientific names of these two corals are *Turbinaria auricularis* (left) and *Pocillopora modumanesis* (right).

Nourished by frequent meals of zooplankton, polyps in a colony are able to reproduce rapidly, adding new members by budding or fission. As a colony grows, its limestone housing takes on the particular shape that is characteristic of the colony members.

Colonies of stony corals grow in strange and varied shapes. Some form massive, boulder-like structures, while others develop branches and limbs that resemble trees. Coral colonies can also grow in the shape of flat plates or shelves.

Each kind of coral has its own characteristic shape, but the growth of a colony is also affected by many outside influences. The position of a coral colony on a reef, the ocean currents that sweep over it—these and other factors help to determine what form a colony will take.

The coral colonies shown on these two pages are closely related, but each has a very different form. Above is staghorn coral, one of the branching corals. Its limestone skeleton resembles the many-pronged antlers of a stag, or male deer.

Staghorn coral is one of the major reef-building corals in areas of shallow water. Its colonies grow rapidly and often form as much as 75 percent of a reef structure. A close relative of the staghorn is elkhorn coral, whose colonies have thicker "antlers" than the delicate staghorns. Elkhorn colonies also form a major part of many reefs.

Both elkhorn and staghorn coral belong to the genus *Acropora*. The two corals on the opposite page are also members of this genus, although they are very different in appearance.

Bush coral (right) has short, stubby branches clustered close together. Plate coral (above) looks just like its name; its colonies are flat and extremely thin. This kind of coral is usually found in deeper water than the branching members of the genus *Acropora.* The flat shape of a plate coral colony allows each polyp to receive adequate light, which is essential to its growth.

Symphyllia recta is one of the many species of brain coral.

Branching corals like the staghorns and the elkhorns usually grow in the shallow water at the top of a reef. Farther down, in the deep water at the base of the reef, the massive, boulder-like corals can be found. One of the most distinctive corals in this group is brain coral.

Brain coral colonies have a distinctive shape because they are formed in an unusual way. When brain coral polyps multiply by budding, they do not build separate limestone cups. Instead, the polyps remain joined together, forming long, wandering rows. These rows are separated from each other by high limestone ridges that provide protection for the soft polyps.

As a brain coral colony grows, it develops into a dome-shaped mass covered by wavy rows of ridges. Its appearance is very much like that of the human brain with its complicated folds and creases.

18

Left: Bouquet flower coral *(Lobophyllia costata)* has a rounded, boulder-like shape. When its polyps come out of their corallites, the colony resembles a bunch of tiny flowers. *Right:* Mushroom coral *(Fungia concinna)* is unusual because it doesn't form colonies. Each large polyp builds a solitary corallite divided by many septa, which look like the ridges on the underside of a mushroom cap.

These photographs show two different kinds of needle coral, both members of the genus *Seriatopora.* Needle coral colonies form thin, delicate branches, with the polyp corallites close together (shown in the enlarged photograph on the left). This kind of coral usually grows in calm water, where its fragile branches are not threatened by strong ocean currents.

The complicated structure of a coral reef is held together by tiny plants called coralline algae.

A typical coral reef includes many colonies of living corals, but the greater part of the reef structure is made up of the limestone shells of colonies whose inhabitants are no longer alive. When coral polyps die, their soft bodies decay, but their hard limestone skeletons remain. As new colonies establish themselves on the rocky foundations left by the dead corals, the reef grows ever larger and more complex.

Because of the disorderly way in which it develops, a

coral reef is a jumble of limestone branches, boulders, and other fantastic shapes. All these separate elements are held together by a kind of "cement" that gives the reef great strength and durability. Much of the reef cement is produced by tiny plants called **coralline algae**. Like coral polyps, the algae have the ability to extract calcium carbonate from sea water. The tiny plants cover the surfaces of the coral skeletons, binding them together with a thin coating of limestone.

Coralline algae are not the only microscopic plants that play an important role in the life of a coral reef. Other algae, known as **zooxanthellae**, exist within the bodies of many coral polyps, living in close partnership with them.

Zooxanthellae are one-celled algae so tiny that they can grow and reproduce inside the cells of the polyps' bodies. Like all plants, zooxanthellae obtain nourishment through photosynthesis, a process that uses the energy of the sun to make food. One of the essential ingredients of photosynthesis is the gas carbon dioxide, which the polyps produce during the process of respiration. The algae use carbon dioxide and other coral waste products in making their own food. In return, the polyps receive oxygen and nutrients produced by the zooxanthellae during photosynthesis.

There are other ways in which zooxanthellae and the polyps aid each other, but scientists do not yet understand the exact details of their relationship. It seems clear, however, that most reef-building stony corals cannot function efficiently without the assistance of their tiny algal partners.

21

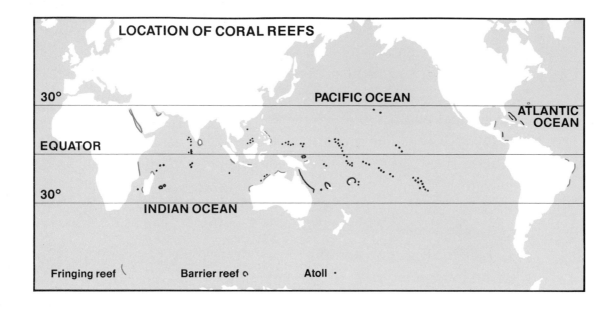

LOCATION OF CORAL REEFS

30°

PACIFIC OCEAN

ATLANTIC OCEAN

EQUATOR

30°

INDIAN OCEAN

Fringing reef   Barrier reef   Atoll

The important role that zooxanthellae play in the lives of reef-building corals is one of the factors that help to determine the locations of coral reefs. Since zooxanthellae require sunlight in order to conduct photosynthesis, they cannot survive in deep ocean water where the sun's rays do not penetrate. In order to accommodate their algal guests, stony corals grow only in shallow water no more than 150 feet (45 meters) deep.

Stony corals have some other requirements in regard to living conditions. They need an environment of water that is clear and warm in order to develop successfully. The only part of the world where all these requirements can be met is the tropical regions extending about 30 degrees on either side of the Equator. It is within this wide band circling the middle of the earth that most coral reefs are found.

Right: A fringing reef surrounding the Japanese island of Okinawa

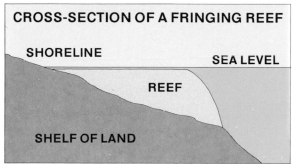

CROSS-SECTION OF A FRINGING REEF

SHORELINE

SEA LEVEL

REEF

SHELF OF LAND

These two drawings show how a fringing reef develops in the shallow water surrounding a land mass.

Because shallow water is necessary for the development of reef-building corals, it is not surprising that many coral reefs are located near bodies of land. **Fringing reefs** grow on the rocky shelves that extend from the shores of islands or continents into the sea. This kind of reef is closely connected to the land, forming a fringe of coral along the shoreline.

Left: A barrier reef around one of the Yap Islands in the western Pacific. This kind of reef is separated from the shore by the calm waters of lagoons.

Another common kind of reef, the **barrier reef**, is separated from the shoreline by areas of shallow water called **lagoons**. Instead of fringing the land, a barrier reef runs parallel to it, forming a division between the rough waters of the open sea and the calm waters of the sheltered lagoons.

The Great Barrier Reef, located off the northeastern coast of Australia, is the world's largest and best known coral reef.

24

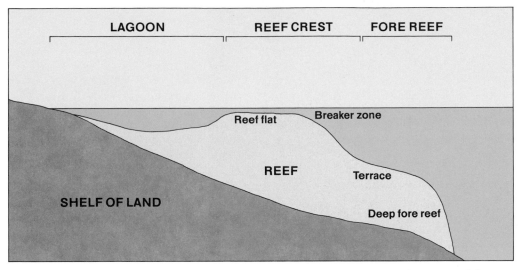

A barrier reef is a complicated structure made up of many different elements. The cross-section drawing above shows some of the parts of a typical barrier reef.

This enormous formation of limestone stretches for more than 1,200 miles (1,920 kilometers) and, at its widest, extends more than 150 miles (241 kilometers) from the shore. Like most large reefs of the barrier type, the Great Barrier Reef is made up of many smaller reefs separated by channels that connect the enclosed lagoons to the open sea. This immense reef complex includes many different environments inhabited by a great variety of living things.

A third major type of coral reef is the **atoll**, and it is the most unusual of all. An atoll is a ring of coral surrounding nothing but water. For many years, scientists were puzzled by these strange coral formations, most of which are located in the deepest parts of the Pacific Ocean, far from any land. The 19th-century scientist Charles Darwin was one of the first to suggest an explanation for the existence of atolls.

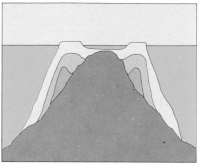

The Pacific atoll of Pakin developed around a volcanic island that became submerged in the sea.

Darwin thought that atolls were old coral reefs that had been growing for long periods of time. They had started out as fringing reefs surrounding islands formed by volcanic eruptions. As the years passed, the islands gradually sank due to changes in the ocean floor. The reefs surrounding the islands sank too, but new sections of reef were continually being formed in the shallow waters on top of the old reefs. These new reefs were of the barrier type, separated from the island shores by lagoons.

When a volcanic island was completely covered by the sea, its reef became a doughnut-shaped atoll surrounding a calm, shallow lagoon. The top layer of the atoll was made up of living coral, but underneath were hundreds of feet of limestone produced by reef-building polyps long dead.

Later scientific studies have shown that Darwin's theory about the origin of atolls was basically correct. An atoll is the final stage in the development of a reef that began its existence as a coral fringe around a volcanic island.

26

Over a period of time, an atoll may develop still further into a coral island covered with a layer of sand formed from the reef limestone. Trees and plants grow on these ring-shaped islands, sprouting from seeds brought by wind and ocean currents or by visiting birds. Shown here is one of the Truk Islands, located in the western Pacific.

With their tentacles extended, the polyps in this colony of soft coral look like delicate flowers.

Fringing reefs, barrier reefs, and atolls all owe their existence to the stony corals whose limestone skeletons make up most of the reef structure. There are also other kinds of corals growing on or near the reef. These are the soft corals, close relatives of the stony corals but without their ability to produce limestone coverings for their soft bodies.

Soft corals, like stony corals, form colonies made up of hundreds of polyps produced by budding or fission. Instead of living in limestone cups, however, the polyps occupy small holes in the soft, rubbery tissue that holds the colony together. A colony of soft coral may be massive or branching and tree-like, but it never achieves the immense size of many stony coral colonies.

28

Leather coral (genus *Sinularia*) is a branching soft coral with a smooth, leathery appearance. The holes in which its polyps live are so small that they are difficult to see.

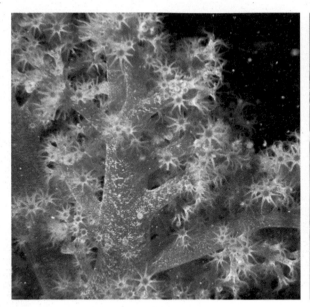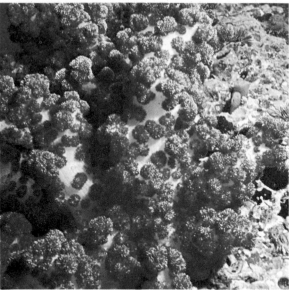

The beautiful soft corals shown above and on the opposite page
are known as glassy tree corals because of their branching shapes
and the transparency of their soft tissue. The needle-like spicules
found in all soft coral colonies can be seen clearly in the photographs above on the left and on the opposite page.

Although soft corals do not produce external limestone
skeletons, they do use limestone to reinforce the rubbery
structure of their colonies. Embedded in the connective
tissue of a soft coral colony are tiny needles of limestone
called **spicules**. Formed from calcium carbonate like the
stony coral skeletons, these spicules strengthen the flexible
material of a soft coral. When the polyps die and the soft
tissue of the colony decays, the hard spicules will eventually
become part of the reef itself, cemented into its jumble of
limestone by coralline algae.

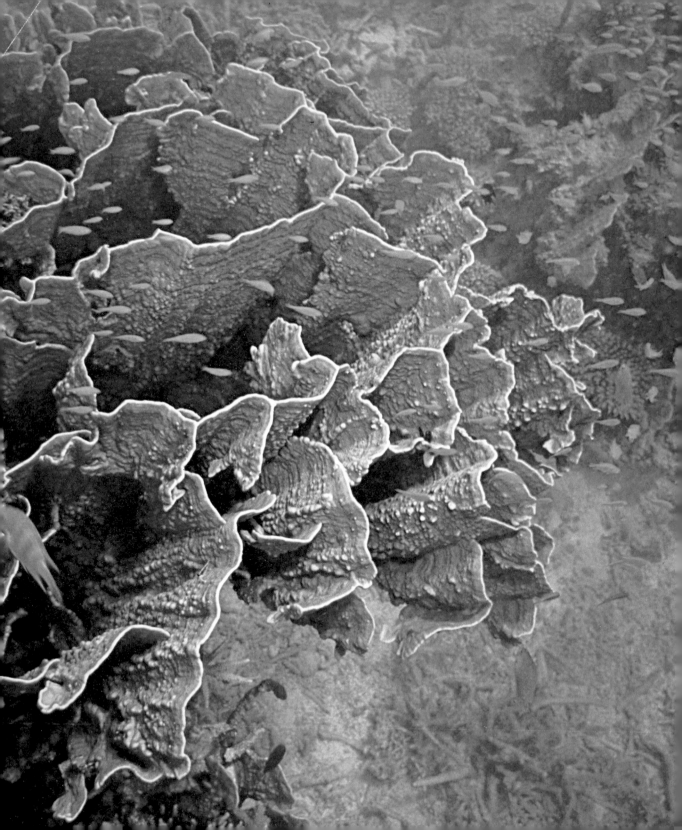

Above: Like all soft corals, this leather coral *(Sarcophyton glaucum)* has polyps with eight tentacles (inset picture). *Left:* Fire coral (genus *Millepora*) belongs to a special group of coelenterates called hydrocorals. Hydrocorals produce hard skeletons like the stony corals, but their polyps live in tiny pores or holes rather than cups. Fire coral gets its common name from the stinging poison of its nematocysts, which is powerful enough to cause painful welts on the skin of human divers.

Gorgonians come in many beautiful colors. This brilliant red species, *Echinogorgia rigida*, spreads its elegant branches in the warm waters of the Pacific.

Some of the most beautiful coral inhabitants of a reef are the gorgonians, whose colonies resemble brightly colored fans, whips, and feathers. Like the soft corals, gorgonians are **octocorals**, with eight tentacles on each of their polyps. Gorgonians also have limestone spicules in their tissues, but they have an additional feature that soft corals lack—an internal skeleton made out of a horn-like material called **gorgonin**.

Because of their flexible skeletons, gorgonians are able to develop colonies made up of long, thin branches that twist and sway in the ocean currents. The name of this unusual group of animals refers to the characteristic shape of these colonies. In Greek mythology, the Gorgons were three sisters whose heads were adorned with living snakes instead of hair.

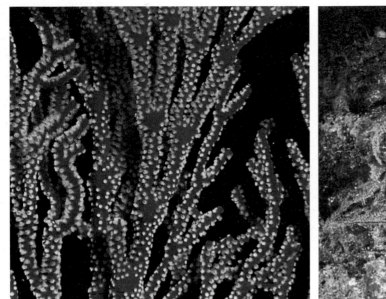

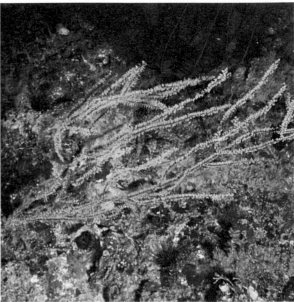

Like all corals, gorgonians are created by colonies of tiny polyps. In these photographs, you can see the polyps that make their homes on the surface of a gorgonian's slender branches.

In addition to the various kinds of corals, many other creatures make their homes in the reef environment. These animals live in the waters around the reef, on the reef structure itself, or on the ocean floor. All are part of the complex community of life in this unique natural setting.

The fat tentacles of this sea anemone *(Actinodendron plumosum)* end in many knobby branches. The anemone's body is buried in the sand.

The sea anemones are among the most distinctive and graceful members of the reef community. Coelenterates like the corals, anemones are giant polyps without the limestone casings of their stony cousins. Their slit-like mouths are surrounded by large numbers of tentacles that can be long and slender or short and stubby. Like the tentacles of coral polyps, these appendages are equipped with stinging nematocysts used to stun and capture food.

Unlike their relatives the corals, most sea anemones live as individuals rather than in colonies, attaching themselves to rocks or burrowing into the sand of the ocean floor. With their stalk-like bodies and brightly colored tentacles, these strange animals resemble the flowers for which they are named.

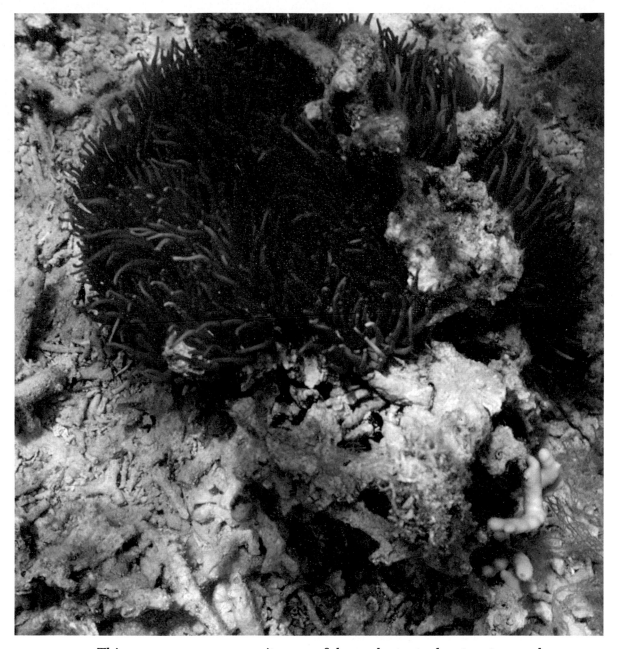

This sea anemone uses its graceful purple tentacles to stun and capture small fish. Other anemones feed on zooplankton or on waste material floating in the ocean waters.

Tube worms on a coral reef extend their colorful tentacles. The species shown here, *Spirobranchus giganteus*, is commonly known as the feather duster worm or the Christmas tree worm because of the strange spiral shape of its tentacles.

Sea anemones hide their true identities by appearing as flowers. Other kinds of reef creatures are concealed under plumes of colorful "feathers." These exotic animals are actually worms, relatives of the common earthworms that tunnel their way through garden soil. Unlike their land-dwelling cousins, the feather-crowned marine worms spend their lives in one place, occupying tubes made out of calcium carbonate or carved into the reef limestone. Because of this unusual living arrangement, they are called tube worms.

The feathery plume that sticks out of a tube worm's home is actually a group of fine tentacles. These tentacles are

Sabellastarte indica is a tube worm with fan-like tentacles.

used both to filter particles of food from the water and to take in oxygen. When the tentacles are not in use, they can be withdrawn inside the tube, along with the rest of the tube worm's body. For extra protection, the entrance to the tube can be covered with the **operculum**, a kind of trap door that seals the worm inside its narrow chamber.

39

Left: Feather stars are echinoderms with long, feathery arms used to gather food from the ocean water. *Right:* The thick, black spines of this echinoderm have earned it the common name slate-pencil sea urchin. Its scientific name is *Heterocentrotus mammillatus.*

Some reef animals do not need to protect themselves with sealed chambers or disguises because their bodies are covered with sharp spines that discourage predators. These animals are called **echinoderms**, a word that means "spiny-skinned."

Echinoderms come in many different shapes and forms. The most distinctive members of the groups are probably the sea stars (sometimes called star fish), whose prickly bodies are usually shaped like five-armed stars. Sea urchins, another common type of echinoderm, have hard, round bodies that resemble pincushions studded with spines.

Sea stars and sea urchins are different in their appearance and in many of their habits, but they have in common an unusual method of locomotion. Both animals walk along on hundreds of tiny **tube feet** tipped with suction disks. The disks grip hard surfaces and enable the echinoderms to move slowly but surely over the reef and the ocean floor.

Some sea stars use these powerful suction disks in obtaining food. The echinoderms feed on oysters, clams, and other mollusks, and they pull open the shells with the aid of the disks on their five "arms." Once the shell is open, the sea star pushes its stomach out through the mouth opening on the lower surface of its body. The stomach enters the shell and surrounds the mollusk's soft body, turning it into food for the sea star's nourishment.

One species of sea star uses this unique method of feeding to attack the soft bodies of coral polyps. This is the crown-of-thorns sea star *(Acanthaster planci)*, a large echinoderm that pushes its stomach into a reef's limestone corallites to reach the polyps hidden inside.

Crown-of-thorns sea stars have enormous appetites and can do great damage to a reef when they feed on it in large numbers. In the 1960s, scientists noticed that the world population of these destructive echinoderms seemed to be increasing rapidly. Large groups of crown-of-thorns were feeding on the Great Barrier Reef and other Pacific reefs, leaving behind them miles of dead coral and crumbling limestone.

This crown-of-thorns sea star is feeding on the polyps of a brain coral.

Since that time, population explosions of the crown-of-thorns have occurred in several areas, causing severe damage. Some scientists believe that these explosions are part of a natural cycle and that the problem will eventually take care of itself. Others think that human interference in the natural world has caused the problem of too many crown-of-thorns. One of the few animals that eat this species of sea star is the triton, a large marine snail with a beautiful striped shell. Shell collectors have reduced the number of tritons in the Pacific, and some scientists believe that this has allowed the crown-of-thorns to increase in number.

Whatever the cause, these bristly echinoderms with their voracious appetites can be very disruptive members of a coral reef community.

Above left: The sharp spines of the long-spined sea urchin *(Diadema setosum)* are equipped with glands containing a poisonous substance. Human divers have learned to avoid this small but dangerous reef animal. *Above right:* This elegant purple and white sea urchin *(Asthenosoma ijimai)* also has poisonous spines.

Left: All sea stars are able to replace lost body parts, but the blue sea star *(Linckia laevigata)* is particularly noted for this ability. The echinoderm can grow a whole new body from a single arm and part of the central disk.

Right: Instead of having five long arms, the pincushion sea star *(Culcita novaeguineae)* is shaped like a pentagon, with five sides to its plump body.

This large clam *(Tridacna elongata)* has its bivalve shell open, revealing its mantle, the fold of tissue that encloses the central part of its body. The small picture shows the clam with its shell closed.

Marine snails like the triton are among the many mollusks that make the reef their home. Snails are **univalve** mollusks, hiding their soft bodies within a single spiralled shell. Many marine snails are fierce predators whose beautifully patterned shells conceal deadly weapons used in taking prey.

The **bivalve**, or two-shelled, mollusks of the reef are much less colorful and conspicuous than their univalve cousins the snails. Clams and oysters often spend their lives half buried in the sand or attached to the reef limestone, opening their shells from time to time to take in water containing particles of food.

Some reef mollusks are conspicuous because of their great size. Giant clams can weigh more than 500 pounds (230 kilograms) and measure 4 feet (1.2 meters) in length. Like their smaller relatives, these enormous mollusks feed only on tiny plants and animals filtered from the sea water.

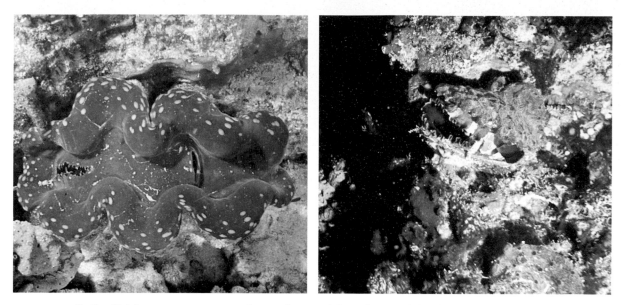

Left: Tridacna squamosa is a clam with a beautiful blue-spotted mantle. A mollusk's mantle produces the shell that protects its soft body. *Right:* The shell of a thorny oyster *(Spondylus varius)* is covered with long spines. This mollusk is often found embedded in the reef limestone.

Left: The cone snail (genus *Conus*) is a predatory marine snail that kills by injecting its prey with a powerful poison. *Right:* The striped triton snail (genus *Charonia*) is also a predator. One of its favorite foods is the destructive crown-of-thorns sea star.

The banded coral shrimp *(Stenopus hispidus)* is one of the "cleaner" shrimps, crustaceans that eat parasites from the bodies of fish.

The crustaceans with their five pairs of armored, jointed legs are also important members of the coral reef community. Spiny lobsters walk along the ocean floor, and tiny shrimps swim through the shallow water around the reef. Crabs with bulging eyes and grasping claws live in the sea and on the sandy shores of coral atolls.

Some crustaceans are notable because of the close relationships they have with other inhabitants of the reef community. Cleaner shrimps like the one shown above perform an essential service for the reef fish and at the same time supply themselves with food. These brightly colored shrimps station themselves at a particular location, often near a sea anemone, and wave their antennae to attract attention. When fish approach, the shrimps form a cleaning crew and eat bothersome parasites from their customers' bodies.

Above: Colorful coral crabs like these live in the crevices of a coral reef. *Below:* The hermit crab is a crustacean that lives in a discarded shell. Unlike other crabs, the hermit has an abdomen that does not have a hard covering like the rest of its body. To protect its abdomen, the crab sticks it inside an old mollusk shell. The shell provides a safe, portable home for this strange reef dweller.

Two elegantly striped butterflyfish *(Chaetodon trifasciatus)* swim past a formation of coral. Butterflyfish often have similar markings on their heads and tails, which may be useful in confusing predators.

Of all the animals that live in the coral reef environment, perhaps the best known are the fish. A reef community is home to hundreds of species of fish of all shapes, sizes, and colors. Tiny, electric-blue damselfish dart through the sunlit waters, while thick grey moray eels hide in the shadows of the reef. Graceful angelfish, sleek barracudas, fat groupers, manta rays with fins like sails—all can be found in the waters around a coral reef.

Like the crustaceans, many fish have close working relationships with other creatures of the reef community. Small fish such as the wrasse perform cleaning duties for larger fish, receiving in return not only food but also the protection of its predatory customers.

Left: Angelfish are closely related to butterflyfish and have the same narrow, streamlined bodies. This is the blue-lined angelfish, *Chaetodontoplus septentrionalis. Right:* The zebra-striped redlip morwong lives in the waters of the western Pacific. Its scientific name is *Goniistius zebra.*

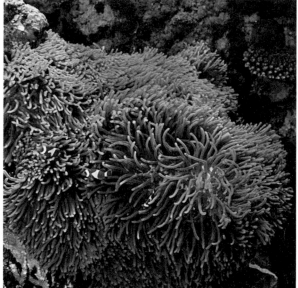

Left: Many of the small, brightly colored fish in the reef community belong to the damselfish family, *Pomacentridae.* This brilliant blue species is *Pomacentrus coelistis,* the heavenly damselfish. *Right:* The gaily striped clown fish *(Amphiprion ocellaris)* is a member of the damselfish family with unusual living habits. This unique fish is described on the following page.

Other kinds of fish find protection in the stinging tentacles of large sea anemones. The little striped clown fish (genus *Amphiprion*) spends most of its life surrounded by an anemone's deadly tentacles, apparently immune to their paralyzing poison. It leaves this formidable shelter only to search for food.

A clown fish finds refuge amid the deadly tentacles of a sea anemone.

Both the clown fish and the anemone benefit from their strange partnership. The anemone gets to eat the left-overs from the fish's meals. Other kinds of fish lured into the anemone's embrace by the presence of the clown fish are also gobbled up. In return for its contributions to the anemone's food supply, the clown fish is protected from predators by its host's dangerous tentacles. Scientists are not sure why the clown fish itself is immune to the anemone's poison. One possibility is that its body is covered with a special mucus that prevents the nematocysts from releasing their poison-tipped threads.

Like the clown fish and the sea anemone, many creatures of the coral reef depend on each other for protection, nourishment, and other essentials of life. They are related to each other as predators and prey, hosts and guests, providers of a service and satisfied customers. No matter what role they play, all the creatures of a coral reef contribute to the intricate balance that maintains the existence of the reef community.

A Note on Scientific Classification

When you are dealing with a large number of things—whether it is a bag of assorted marbles or all the animals in the world—one way to make sense out of the collection is to classify it, or break it up into smaller groups. This is what scientists do when they try to describe the world of nature. They arrange all known animals and plants in groups based on their similarities and their relationships with each other.

The modern system of scientific classification, which was first developed in the 1700s, includes seven basic groups, each one smaller than the one preceding it. The groups are:

Kingdom
Phylum
Class
Order
Family
Genus
Species

Let's take one of the corals pictured in this book through the system of scientific classification so that you can see how it works. The coral shown on the opposite page (and on page 19) is usually known by the common English name bouquet flower coral, but in the system of classification, it is named and described in Latin, a language understood by scientists all over the world.

Like all corals, bouquet flower coral belongs to the animal kingdom—Animalia—which is divided into at least 20 different phyla (the Latin plural of phylum). Corals are members of the phylum Coelenterata or Cnidaria, along with other water-dwelling creatures such as jellyfish and sea anemones. This phylum is broken into 3 classes, and our coral belongs to the class Anthozoa, which includes sea anemones as well as the various types of corals. Anthozoa is further divided into 3 subclasses, one of which, Zoantharia, is made up of sea anemones and stony corals. Since our coral is a stony coral, it belongs in this group.

Order is the next level of classification and Zoantharia includes 2 orders—Actiniaria, the sea anemones, and Scleractinia, the stony corals. Families come next, and now we are talking about groups whose members have many things in common. Our coral is in the family Mussidae, which is made up of dome-shaped corals with large, fleshy polyps and serrated septa. Within this family are 12 genera (the plural of genus), among them *Lobophyllia.* This is the group to which our coral belongs.

The genus *Lobophyllia* includes several species of corals that are commonly called bouquet flower coral, but we are looking for only one species, the coral pictured below. The species name of this coral is *Lobophyllia costata.*

If you can recognize bouquet flower coral by its proper scientific name, then you have taken the first step in learning the language of science and in understanding the system that scientists use to describe the varied inhabitants of the natural world.

GLOSSARY

asexual reproduction—a process of reproduction that does not involve the union of male and female sex cells. Budding is a form of asexual reproduction.

atoll (A-tohl)—a ring-shaped coral reef surrounding a shallow lagoon

barrier reef—a coral reef that runs parallel to the shore and is separated from it by a lagoon

bivalve—a mollusk with a shell composed of two parts, or valves

budding—a form of asexual reproduction in which a new polyp develops as an offshoot from the tissue of an existing polyp

calcium carbonate (KAL-see-um KAR-buhn-ate)—a chemical compound from which limestone is formed

Coelenterata (seh-lent-eh-RAHT-uh)—the scientific group or phylum to which corals, sea anemones, and jellyfish belong. Another name for this phylum is **Cnidaria (ni-DAR-ee-uh),** a word that refers to the stinging cells possessed by corals and their relatives

coral colony—a group of coral polyps living in adjoining corallites and cooperating in carrying on some body processes

coralline algae (KOR-uh-line AHL-jee)—tiny plants that encrust a coral reef, binding its elements together with a coating of limestone

corallite (KOR-uh-lite)—the limestone cup in which a coral polyp lives

echinoderms (ih-KI-nih-derms)—sea stars, sea urchins, and other members of the phylum Echinodermata

fringing reef—a coral reef that forms along the shoreline of a land mass

gorgonin (GOR-guh-nin)—a horn-like material that forms the internal skeletons of gorgonian corals

lagoon (luh-GOON)—an area of shallow water between a barrier reef and the shore or within an atoll

nematocyst (neh-MAD-uh-sist)—a stinging device used by corals and other coelenterates to stun and capture food

octocorals (AHK-teh-kor-uhls)—corals whose polyps have eight tentacles

operculum (o-PER-kyuh-lum)—a plate that covers the opening of a tube worm's tube, sealing the animal inside

planulae (PLAN-yeh-lee)—immature coral polyps. The singular form of the word is **planula.**

septa—the thin limestone plates that divide a corallite. The singular form of the word is **septum.**

sexual reproduction—a form of reproduction in which new life is created by the union of male and female sex cells

spicules (SPIK-yuhls)—tiny needles of limestone that support the tissues of soft corals

stony corals—corals that produce external limestone skeletons

tentacles (TENT-ih-kuhls)—flexible, tube-like body parts surrounding the mouth openings of coral polyps and other coelenterates, used to collect food

tube feet—tube-shaped projections tipped with suction disks, used by echinoderms in walking or grasping objects

univalve—a mollusk with a single, undivided shell

zooplankton (zo-eh-PLANK-tun)—the mass of tiny animals floating in the ocean or other bodies of water. Zooplankton includes one-celled animals and immature forms of sea creatures such as crustaceans.

zooxanthellae (zo-eh-zan-THEL-ee)—one-celled algae that live inside the bodies of coral polyps. The singular form of the word is **zooxanthella.**

INDEX